100 QUOTES TO KEEP YOU GOING ON YOUR JOB SEARCH

Miriam Figueroa

Asha Publisher

AUTHOR'S NOTE

◆ ◆ ◆

Thank you for picking up "100 Quotes to Keep You Going on Your Job Search." This book is a culmination of my own experiences and struggles in the job market. After being laid off in 2024, I learned the importance of staying motivated and persistent. I hope these quotes provide you with the encouragement and strength you need on your journey.

HOW TO USE THIS BOOK

◆ ◆ ◆

This book is designed to be a source of daily inspiration. Whether you're just starting your job search or have been on the journey for a while, these quotes are meant to uplift and motivate you. Feel free to read through it sequentially or jump to the quotes that resonate with you most on any given day.

INTRODUCTION AND MOTIVATION

◆ ◆ ◆

Searching for a job can be one of the most challenging endeavors we face in life. It requires resilience in the face of rejection, the ability to market oneself effectively, and the skill to make a lasting impression in just a few seconds. This book, "100 Quotes to Keep You Going on Your Job Search," aims to provide the motivation and encouragement you need during this journey.

Humorously, someone once compared the job search to a dating app: you put your best self forward and hope for a match. While this comparison may seem amusing, it holds a grain of truth. Like a tennis match where players need constant motivation, the job search requires persistence and a positive mindset. Unlike a tennis match, however, a job search can result in a win-win situation for both the employer and the candidate, where both parties find the right fit.

The process is undoubtedly stressful for both sides. Employers need to select the right candidate who will grow with the company, while candidates hope to find a place where they can thrive. This dual pressure makes the journey tough, but it also underscores the importance of staying motivated.

I decided to compile these quotes to brighten your day and remind you that each day brings new opportunities. Even in the face of rejection, it's essential to stay grateful and hopeful. Trust that God has a plan for you and will guide you to the right job.

In 2024, I was laid off and faced my own difficult journey of job searching. Despite my efforts—reading numerous books, expanding my network, and seeking advice—I struggled to find a new position. I realized that my struggles were not a reflection of my worth, but rather a symptom of the broader economic climate. This realization inspired me to share my experiences and motivations with you.

This book is not about providing job search strategies or tips. Instead, it's about offering encouragement and sharing the lessons I've learned along the way. Here are eight key insights I wish I had known before being laid off:

1. **Keep Your Resume Updated**: Always keep your resume current and continuously improve your skills.
2. **Expand Your Network:** Build a strong network for potential referrals, though not everyone may provide them.
3. **Maintain Emergency Funds:** Review your expenses and ensure you have a safety net.
4. **Lean on Family:** Your support system is crucial during tough times.
5. **Focus on Onsite, Hybrid, and Remote Jobs:** If you've been working remotely, consider applying for onsite or hybrid positions due to the high competition for remote jobs.
6. **Share Your Experiences:** Talking with friends and family can provide motivation and support.
7. **Apply Consistently:** Create a routine for applying and improving your interview skills.
8. **Take Control of Your Finances:** Manage your

investments wisely, especially if converting accounts after job loss.

Through these insights and the quotes within this book, I hope to provide you with the encouragement you need to keep going, even on the toughest days. Remember, every setback is a setup for a greater comeback.

LIST OF QUOTES

1. Keep going, your persistence will pay off.
2. Every application is a step closer to your dream job.
3. Keep searching for what ignites your passion.
4. Confidence in yourself is key to finding the right opportunity.
5. Stay focused and keep moving forward, regardless of how long the process takes. Persistence is key.
6. Take charge of your job search and actively create the opportunities you want to see.
7. Your hard work will lead to something great.
8. Aim high and take bold steps towards your goals.
9. Keep striving, the finish line is closer than you think.
10. Believe in your potential and keep moving forward.
11. Resilience is crucial. Bounce back from setbacks stronger and more determined.
12. Take control of your job search and shape your destiny.
13. Don't fear failure, embrace it as a part of your journey.
14. Stay focused and success will follow.
15. Hard work increases your chances of finding the right job.
16. Take risks to achieve extraordinary outcomes.
17. Challenge yourself and grow through your job search.
18. Keep pushing your boundaries.
19. Begin with the resources and skills you have now. Every small effort counts towards your success.
20. Focus on the present and the future.
21. Take action and start applying for jobs. The first step is often the hardest, but it's the beginning of your journey.

22. Stay focused and determined.
23. Be proactive in your job search.
24. Don't be afraid to take chances.
25. Begin your journey and success will follow.
26. Start now and greatness will come.
27. Grow through your job search.
28. Believe in yourself and your abilities.
29. Work hard and success will follow.
30. Embrace hard work as a path to success.
31. Create your own opportunities.
32. Let your success speak for itself.
33. Put in the work and your dreams will come true.
34. Stay committed to your journey.
35. Focus on becoming the best version of yourself.
36. Stay positive and optimistic.
37. It's never too late to pursue your dreams.
38. Take initiative and create opportunities.
39. Believe in your potential.
40. Stay persistent; success might be just around the corner.
41. Take control of your career path.
42. Keep moving forward, no matter the pace.
43. Persist through challenges.
44. Find fulfillment in your work.
45. Dream big and take action.
46. Embrace the excitement of achieving your goals.
47. Take every opportunity that comes your way.
48. Begin your journey and success will follow.
49. Set goals and work towards them diligently.
50. Take control of your career path.
51. Keep moving forward, no matter the pace.
52. Let your success speak for itself.
53. Dream big and take action.
54. Embrace the excitement of achieving your goals.
55. Take every opportunity that comes your way.

56. Change your narrative and unlock your potential.
57. Set goals and work towards them diligently.
58. Take control of your career path.
59. Keep your spirits high and continue striving.
60. Every failure is a step closer to success.
61. Stay courageous and resilient.
62. When the job search feels overwhelming, turn to Jesus for rest and renewal. Trust that He will provide the strength you need.
63. Seek Jesus as your guide during your job search. His truth and direction can lead you to the right opportunities.
64. Remember that even when a job search seems daunting, with faith in God, all things are possible.
65. In the midst of uncertainty and job search stress, Jesus offers peace. Trust in His peace to calm your fears.
66. Let Jesus' light guide you through the dark moments of job searching, illuminating your path to new opportunities.
67. Know that Jesus is with you throughout your job search journey, providing support and encouragement every step of the way.
68. Despite the challenges and rejections you may face, take heart in knowing Jesus has overcome the world and offers you peace.
69. Trust in God's provision and focus on doing your best in your job search. He will take care of your needs.
70. Persist in your job search with faith. Ask for guidance, seek opportunities, and knock on doors, trusting that they will open.
71. Jesus wants you to have a fulfilling life. Keep striving for a job that not only meets your needs but also brings you joy and purpose.
72. Trust in your abilities and potential.
73. Focus on finding a job that truly fulfills you. Don't settle for anything less than what you deserve.
74. Pursue a career that brings you joy. When you are happy, success will naturally follow.
75. Don't be afraid to take risks and aim high. Every failure is a step closer to success.
76. No matter where you are in your career, it's never too late to pursue your dreams and achieve your goals.
77. Embrace the challenges you face. They are preparing you for a remarkable future.

78. Treat your job search as a series of small, manageable steps. Each step brings you closer to your goal.

79. Look for the silver lining in challenging situations. Difficulties often lead to new and exciting opportunities.

80. Your inner strength and character are your greatest assets. Believe in yourself and your capabilities.

81. Every application, interview, and follow-up counts. Your efforts are making a significant impact.

82. The more challenging the journey, the sweeter the victory. Keep pushing through.

83. Sometimes the best opportunities are closer than you think. Stay alert and open to possibilities.

84. Let your determination be your driving force. With unwavering resolve, you will succeed.

85. Utilize your current skills and resources to the best of your ability. Progress comes from consistent effort.

86. It's not about avoiding failure, but about rising each time you fall. Keep getting back up.

87. Resilience is key. Each time you get back up, you become stronger and more prepared for success.

88. Confidence is half the battle. Believe in yourself and your abilities to achieve your goals.

89. Have faith in the possibility of success. Your belief can turn the impossible into reality.

90. Focus on the present and future, and let go of past setbacks.

91. Trust in His peace to calm your fears.

92. Use your imagination to visualize your career goals. Dreaming is the first step in planning your path to success.

93. Don't be afraid to pivot or try something new in your job search. You have the power to redefine your career path at any moment.

94. Start your job search now, even if you don't feel completely prepared. Taking action is better than waiting for the perfect moment.

95. Act on your ideas and take concrete steps towards your job goals. Turning ideas into action is what sets you apart.

96. Embrace discomfort as a catalyst for change. Use it to push yourself out of your comfort zone and explore new job opportunities.

97. Take control of your job search with confidence and

determination. Don't let obstacles deter you from achieving your goals.

98. Be proactive in your job search. You have the power to create the change you want to see in your career.

99. View setbacks as opportunities to learn and grow. Each challenge makes you stronger and more resilient.

100. Be relentless in your pursuit of job opportunities. Persistence and determination will help you achieve your career goals.

1. Keep going, your persistence will pay off.

"Success is not final, failure is not fatal: It is the courage to continue that counts."

– Winston Churchill.

2. Every application is a step closer to your dream job.

"The future depends on what you do today."

- Mahatma Gandhi.

3. Keep searching for what ignites your passion.

"The only way to do great work is to love what you do."

- Steve Jobs.

4. Confidence in yourself is key to finding the right opportunity.

"Believe you can and you're halfway there."

- Theodore Roosevelt.

5. Stay focused and keep moving forward, regardless of how long the process takes. Persistence is key.

"Don't watch the clock; do what it does. Keep going."

- Sam Levenson.

6. Take charge of your job search and actively create the opportunities you want to see.

"Opportunities don't happen, you create them."

- Chris Grosser.

---

7. Your hard work will lead to something great.

"The harder you work for something, the greater you'll feel when you achieve it."

- Unknown.

8. Aim high and take bold steps towards your goals.

"Don't be afraid to give up the good to go for the great."

- John D. Rockefeller.

9. Keep striving, the finish line is closer than you think.

"It always seems impossible until it's done."

- Nelson Mandela.

---

10. Believe in your potential and keep moving forward.

"The only limit to our realization of tomorrow is our doubts of today."

- Franklin D. Roosevelt.

11. Resilience is crucial. Bounce back from setbacks stronger and more determined.

"Success is how high you bounce when you hit bottom."

- George S. Patton.

12. Take control of your job search and shape your destiny.

"The best way to predict the future is to create it."

- Abraham Lincoln.

13. Don't fear failure, embrace it as a part of your journey.

"Dream big and dare to fail."

- Norman Vaughan

14. Stay focused and success will follow.

"Success usually comes to those who are too busy to be looking for it."

- Henry David Thoreau.

15. Hard work increases your chances of finding the right job.

"I find that the harder I work, the more luck I seem to have."

- Thomas Jefferson.

16. Take risks to achieve extraordinary outcomes.

"If you are not willing to risk the usual, you will have to settle for the ordinary."

- Jim Rohn.

17. Challenge yourself and grow through your job search.

"Do one thing every day that scares you."

- Eleanor Roosevelt.

18. Keep pushing your boundaries.

"Go as far as you can see; when you get there, you'll be able to see further."

– Thomas Carlyle.

19. Begin with the resources and skills you have now. Every small effort counts towards your success.

"Start where you are. Use what you have. Do what you can."

- Arthur Ashe.

20. Focus on the present and the future.

"Don't let yesterday take up too much of today."

- Will Rogers.

21. Take action and start applying for jobs. The first step is often the hardest, but it's the beginning of your journey.

"The way to get started is to quit talking and begin doing."

- Walt Disney.

22. Stay focused and determined.

"The successful warrior is the average man, with laser-like focus."

- Bruce Lee.

23. Be proactive in your job search.

"Don't wait for opportunity. Create it."

- George Bernard Shaw.

24.   Don't be afraid to take chances.

"The biggest risk is not taking any risk."

- Mark Zuckerberg.

25. Begin your journey and success will follow.

"The secret of getting ahead is getting started".

– Mark Twain.

26. Start now and greatness will come.

"You don't have to be great to start, but you have to start to be great."

– Zig Ziglar.

27. Grow through your job search.

"What you get by achieving your goals is not as important as what you become by achieving your goals."

– Zig Ziglar.

28. Believe in yourself and your abilities.

"In order to succeed, we must first believe that we can."

– Nikos Kazantzakis.

29. Work hard and success will follow.

"The only place where success comes before work is in the dictionary."

– Vidal Sassoon.

30. Embrace hard work as a path to success.

"Opportunities are usually disguised as hard work, so most people don't recognize them."

– Ann Landers.

31. Create your own opportunities.

"If opportunity doesn't knock, build a door."

– Milton Berle.

32. Let your success speak for itself.

"The best revenge is massive success."

– Frank Sinatra

33. Put in the work and your dreams will come true.

"I never dreamed about success, I worked for it."

– Estée Lauder.

34. Stay committed to your journey.

"There are no shortcuts to any place worth going."

– Beverly Sills.

35. Focus on becoming the best version of yourself.

"Success is not in what you have, but who you are."

– Bo Bennett.

36. Stay positive and optimistic.

"Keep your face always toward the sunshine—and shadows will fall behind you."

– Walt Whitman.

37.   It's never too late to pursue your dreams.

"You are never too old to set another goal or to dream a new dream."

– C.S. Lewis.

38. Take initiative and create opportunities.

"Do not wait to strike till the iron is hot, but make it hot by striking."

– William Butler Yeats.

39. Believe in your potential.

"The only way to achieve the impossible is to believe it is possible."

– Charles Kingsleigh.

40. Stay persistent; success might be just around the corner.

"Many of life's failures are people who did not realize how close they were to success when they gave up."

– Thomas A. Edison.

---

41.   Take control of your career path.

"The best way to predict your future is to create it."

– Peter Drucker.

42. Keep moving forward, no matter the pace.

"It does not matter how slowly you go as long as you do not stop."

– Confucius.

43. Persist through challenges.

"Success is not the absence of failure; it's the persistence through failure."

– Aisha Tyler.

44. Find fulfillment in your work.

"Success is liking yourself, liking what you do, and liking how you do it."

– Maya Angelou.

45. Dream big and take action.

"If you can dream it, you can do it."

– Walt Disney.

46. Embrace the excitement of achieving your goals.

"Don't let the fear of losing be greater than the excitement of winning."

– Robert Kiyosaki.

47. Take every opportunity that comes your way.

"You miss 100% of the shots you don't take."

– Wayne Gretzky.

48. Begin your journey and success will follow.

The secret of getting ahead is getting started."

- Mark Twain.

49. Set goals and work towards them diligently.

"A goal is a dream with a deadline."

– Napoleon Hill.

50. Take control of your career path.

"The best way to predict your future is to create it."

– Peter Drucker.

51. Keep moving forward, no matter the pace.

"It does not matter how slowly you go as long as you do not stop."

– Confucius.

52. Let your success speak for itself.

"The best revenge is massive success."

– Frank Sinatra.

53. Dream big and take action.

"If you can dream it, you can do it."

– Walt Disney.

54. Embrace the excitement of achieving your goals.

"Don't let the fear of losing be greater than the excitement of winning."

– Robert Kiyosaki.

55. Take every opportunity that comes your way.

"You miss 100% of the shots you don't take."

– Wayne Gretzky.

56. Change your narrative and unlock your potential.

"The only thing standing between you and your goal is the story you keep telling yourself as to why you can't achieve it."

– Jordan Belfort.

57. Set goals and work towards them diligently.

"A goal is a dream with a deadline."

– Napoleon Hill.

58. Take control of your career path.

"The best way to predict your future is to create it."

– Peter Drucker.

59. Keep your spirits high and continue striving.

"Success is stumbling from failure to failure with no loss of enthusiasm."

– Winston S. Churchill.

60. Every failure is a step closer to success.

"Perseverance is failing 19 times and succeeding the 20th."

– Julie Andrews.

61. Stay courageous and resilient.

"Success is not measured by what you accomplish, but by the opposition you have encountered, and the courage with which you have maintained the struggle against overwhelming odds."

– Orison Swett Marden.

62. When the job search feels overwhelming, turn to Jesus for rest and renewal. Trust that He will provide the strength you need.

"Come to me, all you who are weary and burdened, and I will give you rest."

– Matthew 11:28.

63. Seek Jesus as your guide during your job search. His truth and direction can lead you to the right opportunities.

"I am the way and the truth and the life. No one comes to the Father except through me."

– John 14:6.

64. Remember that even when a job search seems daunting, with faith in God, all things are possible.

"With man this is impossible, but with God all things are possible."

– Matthew 19:26.

65. In the midst of uncertainty and job search stress, Jesus offers peace. Trust in His peace to calm your fears.

"Peace I leave with you; my peace I give you. I do not give to you as the world gives. Do not let your hearts be troubled and do not be afraid."

– John 14:27.

66. Let Jesus' light guide you through the dark moments of job searching, illuminating your path to new opportunities.

"I am the light of the world. Whoever follows me will never walk in darkness, but will have the light of life." – John 8:12.

---

67. Know that Jesus is with you throughout your job search journey, providing support and encouragement every step of the way.

"And surely I am with you always, to the very end of the age."

– Matthew 28:20.

68. Despite the challenges and rejections you may face, take heart in knowing Jesus has overcome the world and offers you peace.

"I have told you these things, so that in me you may have peace. In this world you will have trouble. But take heart! I have overcome the world."

– John 16:33.

69. Trust in God's provision and focus on doing your best in your job search. He will take care of your needs.

"Therefore I tell you, do not worry about your life, what you will eat or drink; or about your body, what you will wear. Is not life more than food, and the body more than clothes?"

– Matthew 6:25

70. Persist in your job search with faith. Ask for guidance, seek opportunities, and knock on doors, trusting that they will open.

"Ask and it will be given to you; seek and you will find; knock and the door will be opened to you."

– Matthew 7:7.

71. Jesus wants you to have a fulfilling life. Keep striving for a job that not only meets your needs but also brings you joy and purpose.

The thief comes only to steal and kill and destroy; I have come that they may have life, and have it to the full."

– John 10:10.

72. Trust in your abilities and potential.

Remember that you have the strength to overcome any challenge that comes your way.

"Believe in yourself and all that you are. Know that there is something inside you that is greater than any obstacle."

- Christian D. Larson

---

73. Focus on finding a job that truly fulfills you. Don't settle for anything less than what you deserve.

"Your time is limited, so don't waste it living someone else's life."

- Steve Jobs

74. Pursue a career that brings you joy. When you are happy, success will naturally follow.

"Success is not the key to happiness. Happiness is the key to success."

- Albert Schweitzer

75. Don't be afraid to take risks and aim high. Every failure is a step closer to success.

"Dream big and dare to fail."

- Norman Vaughan

76. No matter where you are in your career, it's never too late to pursue your dreams and achieve your goals.

"It's never too late to be what you might have been"

- George Eliot."

77. Embrace the challenges you face. They are preparing you for a remarkable future.

"Hardships often prepare ordinary people for an extraordinary destiny."

- C.S. Lewis.

78. Treat your job search as a series of small, manageable steps. Each step brings you closer to your goal.

"Perseverance is not a long race; it is many short races one after the other."

- Walter Elliot.

79. Look for the silver lining in challenging situations. Difficulties often lead to new and exciting opportunities.

"In the middle of every difficulty lies opportunity."

- Albert Einstein

80. Your inner strength and character are your greatest assets. Believe in yourself and your capabilities.

"What lies behind us and what lies before us are tiny matters compared to what lies within us."

- Ralph Waldo Emerson

81. Every application, interview, and follow-up counts. Your efforts are making a significant impact.

"Act as if what you do makes a difference. It does."

- William James.

82. The more challenging the journey, the sweeter the victory. Keep pushing through.

"The harder the conflict, the more glorious the triumph."

- Thomas Paine

---

83. Sometimes the best opportunities are closer than you think. Stay alert and open to possibilities.

"Your big opportunity may be right where you are now."

- Napoleon Hill

84. Let your determination be your driving force. With unwavering resolve, you will succeed.

"Failure will never overtake me if my determination to succeed is strong enough."

- Og Mandino

85. Utilize your current skills and resources to the best of your ability. Progress comes from consistent effort.

"Do what you can, with what you have, where you are."

- Theodore Roosevelt.

86. It's not about avoiding failure, but about rising each time you fall. Keep getting back up.

"Our greatest glory is not in never falling, but in rising every time we fall."

- Confucius

87. Resilience is key. Each time you get back up, you become stronger and more prepared for success.

"It's not whether you get knocked down, it's whether you get up."

- Vince Lombardi.

88. Confidence is half the battle. Believe in yourself and your abilities to achieve your goals.

"Believe you can and you're halfway there."

- Theodore Roosevelt

89. Have faith in the possibility of success. Your belief can turn the impossible into reality.

"The only way to achieve the impossible is to believe it is possible."

- Charles Kingsleigh.

90. Focus on the present and future, and let go of past setbacks.

"Do not let yesterday take up too much of today."

– Will Rogers

91. Trust in His peace to calm your fears.

"Peace I leave with you; my peace I give you. I do not give to you as the world gives. Do not let your hearts be troubled and do not be afraid."

– John 14:27

92. Use your imagination to visualize your career goals. Dreaming is the first step in planning your path to success.

"Without leaps of imagination or dreaming, we lose the excitement of possibilities. Dreaming, after all, is a form of planning."

– Gloria Steinem

93. Don't be afraid to pivot or try something new in your job search. You have the power to redefine your career path at any moment.

"You are always free to change your mind and choose a different future, or a different past."

– Richard Bach

94. Start your job search now, even if you don't feel completely prepared. Taking action is better than waiting for the perfect moment.

"If we wait for the moment when everything, absolutely everything is ready, we shall never begin."

– Ivan Turgenev

95. Act on your ideas and take concrete steps towards your job goals. Turning ideas into action is what sets you apart.

"Everyone who's ever taken a shower has an idea. It's the person who gets out of the shower, dries off and does something about it who makes a difference."

– Nolan Bushnell

96. Embrace discomfort as a catalyst for change. Use it to push yourself out of your comfort zone and explore new job opportunities.

The truth is that our finest moments are most likely to occur when we are feeling deeply uncomfortable, unhappy or unfulfilled. For it is only in such moments, propelled by our discomfort, that we are likely to step out of our ruts and start searching for different ways or truer answers."

– M. Scott Peck

97. Take control of your job search with confidence and determination. Don't let obstacles deter you from achieving your goals.

"The question isn't who is going to let me. It's who is going to stop me."

– Ayn Rand

98. Be proactive in your job search. You have the power to create the change you want to see in your career.

"Change will not come if we wait for some other person or some other time. We are the ones we've been waiting for. We are the change that we seek."

– Barack Obama

99. View setbacks as opportunities to learn and grow. Each challenge makes you stronger and more resilient.

You may encounter many defeats, but you must not be defeated. In fact, it may be necessary to encounter the defeats, so you can know who you are, what you can rise from, how you can still come out of it."

– Maya Angelou

100. Be relentless in your pursuit of job opportunities. Persistence and determination will help you achieve your career goals.

"Where there is a will, there is a way. If there is a chance in a million that you can do something, anything, to keep what you want from ending, do it. Pry the door open or, if need be, wedge your foot in that door and keep it open."

– Pauline Kael

WORDS OF ENCOURAGEMENT

1. **Keep Faith in Yourself:** Remember that every job application brings you one step closer to your dream job. Believe in your skills and stay confident.
2. **Stay Positive:** Rejections are not a reflection of your worth. Each "no" gets you closer to a "yes." Keep a positive mindset.
3. **Lean on Support:** Don't hesitate to reach out to friends, family, or mentors for support and advice. Their encouragement can be a great boost.
4. **Stay Organized:** Keeping track of your applications can help you stay on top of your job search and reduce stress.
5. **Learn and Adapt:** Every interview and application is a learning opportunity. Reflect on what went well and what can be improved.

JOB APPLICATION TRACKER TEMPLATE

Company Name	Position	Date Applied	Contact Person	Follow-up Date	Status	Notes
Example Co.	Marketing Manager	05/01/2024	John Doe	05/08/2024	Interview Scheduled	

How to use:

- **Company Name:** Name of the company you applied to.
- **Position:** Job title you applied for.
- **Date Applied:** The date you submitted your application.
- **Contact Person:** The person you communicated with (if any).
- **Follow-up Date:** When you plan to follow up on your application.
- **Status:** Current status (e.g., applied, interviewed, rejected, offered).
- **Notes:** Any additional notes (e.g., impressions, feedback received).

LIST OF THINGS TO DO WHEN YOU FEEL DOWN

1. **Take a Break:** Step away from job searching for a bit. Go for a walk, read a book, or engage in a hobby.
2. **Exercise:** Physical activity can boost your mood and reduce stress.
3. **Talk to Someone:** Share your feelings with a friend or family member.
4. **Practice Self-care:** Take time for activities that make you feel good, like a bath, meditation, or a good meal.
5. **Reflect on Achievements:** Remind yourself of past accomplishments and strengths.
6. **Set Small Goals:** Break down tasks into smaller, manageable steps.
7. **Stay Positive:** Read inspirational quotes or stories of others who found success after challenges.

WEBSITES TO FIND JOBS

1. **LinkedIn** (www.linkedin.com): Great for networking and finding job postings.
2. **Indeed** (www.indeed.com): One of the largest job search engines.
3. **Glassdoor** (www.glassdoor.com): Provides job listings and company reviews.
4. **Monster** (www.monster.com): Extensive job listings and career advice.
5. **CareerBuilder** (www.careerbuilder.com): Comprehensive job search platform.
6. **SimplyHired** (www.simplyhired.com): Job search engine that aggregates listings from various sources.
7. **FlexJobs** (www.flexjobs.com): Specializes in remote and flexible jobs.
8. **AngelList** (www.angel.co): Focuses on startup job opportunities.
9. **USAJobs** (www.usajobs.gov): Official job site of the U.S. federal government.

ADDITIONAL RESOURCES:

- **Jobscan** (www.jobscan.com): Optimize your resume for applicant tracking systems.

- **Meetup** (www.meetup.com): Find networking events in your area.

RED FLAGS WHEN APPLYING FOR JOBS

1. **Requests for Personal Information:** Be wary if asked for sensitive information (e.g., bank details, Social Security number) before an offer is made.
2. **Lack of Company Information:** If the company has no online presence or credible reviews, it might be a scam.
3. **Unprofessional Communication:** Poor grammar, urgent demands, or unprofessional emails can be a warning sign.
4. **Too Good to Be True:** Be cautious of job offers that promise unusually high salaries for minimal work.
5. **Immediate Job Offers:** Offers made without an interview process are suspect.
6. **Upfront Payments:** Legitimate employers will never ask you to pay for anything upfront.
7. **High-Pressure Tactics:** If you're being pressured to accept a job offer quickly, it might be a scam.

ADDITIONAL TIPS

- ✓ **Tailor Your Resume:** Customize your resume for each job application to highlight relevant skills and experiences.

- ✓ **Prepare for Interviews:** Research the company and practice common interview questions.

- ✓ **Network:** Attend industry events, join professional groups, and connect with people on LinkedIn.

- ✓ **Follow-Up:** After an interview, send a thank-you note to express your appreciation and reiterate your interest.

- ✓ **Stay Updated:** Keep your skills and knowledge current through courses, certifications, and reading industry news.

PRACTICAL JOB SEARCH TIPS

Resume Writing Tips
- ✓ Tailor your resume for each application.
- ✓ Highlight key skills and achievements.
- ✓ Keep it concise and relevant.

Interview Preparation
- ✓ Research the company thoroughly.
- ✓ Practice common interview questions.
- ✓ Dress appropriately and be punctual.

Networking Strategies
- ✓ Attend industry events and job fairs.
- ✓ Reach out to former colleagues and mentors.
- ✓ Join professional groups and associations.

SAMPLE FOLLOW-UP EMAIL TEMPLATE

Subject: Follow-Up on [Position] Application

Dear [Contact Person's Name],

I hope this message finds you well. I wanted to follow up on my application for the [Position] role at [Company Name], which I submitted on [Date]. I am very excited about the opportunity to contribute to your team and would like to inquire about the status of my application.

Please let me know if there are any additional materials or information I can provide. I look forward to the possibility of discussing how my background, skills, and enthusiasm align with the needs of your team.

Thank you for your time and consideration.

Best regards,
[Your Name]
[Your Contact Information]

GENERAL JOB APPLICATION COVER LETTER TEMPLATE

[Your Name]
[Your Address]
[City, State, ZIP Code]
[Your Email Address]
[Your Phone Number]
[Date]

[Hiring Manager's Name]
[Company Name]
[Company Address]
City, State, ZIP Code]

Dear [Hiring Manager's Name],

I am writing to express my interest in any suitable positions within your esteemed company. With [number] years of experience in [your industry or field], I have developed a comprehensive skill set and a deep understanding of [specific areas of expertise]. I am eager to bring my background in [specific skills or experience] to a dynamic organization like [Company Name].

In my previous role at [Your Previous Company], I was responsible for [brief description of your duties]. My ability to [mention a key skill or achievement] has allowed me to contribute significantly to [a specific outcome or project]. I am particularly drawn to [Company Name] because of [specific reason related to company values, culture, or mission].

I am confident that my background, skills, and enthusiasm make me a strong candidate for a position at [Company Name]. I look forward to the opportunity to discuss how my experience and abilities align with the needs of your team.

Thank you for considering my application. I hope to hear from you soon to discuss how I can contribute to the success of [Company Name].

Sincerely,
[Your Name]

SPECIFIC JOB POSTING COVER LETTER TEMPLATE

[Your Name]
[Your Address]
[City, State, ZIP Code]
[Your Email Address]
[Your Phone Number]
[Date]

[Hiring Manager's Name]
[Company Name]
[Company Address]
City, State, ZIP Code

Dear [Hiring Manager's Name],

I am writing to apply for the [Job Title] position at [Company Name], as advertised on [where you found the job posting]. With a background in [your field or industry], and [number] years of experience in [specific role or skill], I am excited about the opportunity to contribute to your team.

At [Your Previous Company], I was responsible for [brief description of your duties and achievements]. I successfully [specific accomplishment], which resulted in [specific outcome]. I am particularly skilled in [mention key skills relevant to the job posting], and I am confident that my expertise aligns with the requirements outlined in your job posting.

I am particularly drawn to [Company Name] because of [specific reason related to the job or company]. I am enthusiastic about the prospect of bringing my [mention any unique skills or perspectives] to your team and contributing to [specific aspect of the company's work].

Thank you for considering my application. I look forward to the opportunity to discuss how my skills and experiences match the needs of your team. I am available at your earliest convenience for an interview.

Sincerely,
[Your Name]

REFERRAL COVER LETTER TEMPLATE

[Your Name]
[Your Address]
[City, State, ZIP Code]
[Your Email Address]
[Your Phone Number]
[Date]

[Hiring Manager's Name]
[Company Name]
[Company Address]
City, State, ZIP Code]

Dear [Hiring Manager's Name],

I am writing to apply for the [Job Title] position at [Company Name], which was recommended to me by [Referrer's Name], who is [explain your relationship with the referrer, e.g., a colleague, mentor, friend]. With [number] years of experience in [your field or industry], I am excited about the opportunity to bring my skills and experiences to your esteemed company.

At [Your Previous Company], I excelled in [brief description of your duties and achievements]. My role involved [specific responsibilities], where I [specific accomplishment]. I believe my skills in [mention key skills relevant to the job] would be a valuable addition to your team.

[Referrer's Name] spoke highly of [Company Name]'s [specific reason related to company values, culture, or mission], and I am particularly drawn to this opportunity because [specific reason you are interested in the job or company]. I am eager to bring my [mention any unique skills or perspectives] to your team and contribute to [specific aspect of the company's work].

Thank you for considering my application. I would welcome the chance to discuss how my background, skills, and enthusiasm can contribute to the success of [Company Name]. I am available for an interview at your earliest convenience.

Sincerely,
[Your Name]

CONCLUSION

Thank you for reading "100 Quotes to Keep You Going on Your Job Search." Remember, every step you take brings you closer to your dream job. Stay motivated, stay persistent, and trust that the right opportunity is out there waiting for you.

Wishing you all the best on your journey.

Miriam Figueroa

APPENDIX

1. **Albert Einstein:** "In the middle of every difficulty lies opportunity." – *Quote #79*

2. **Albert Schweitzer:** "Success is not the key to happiness. Happiness is the key to success." – *Quote #74*

3. **Aisha Tyler:** "Success is not the absence of failure; it's the persistence through failure." – *Quote #43*

4. **Ann Landers:** "Opportunities are usually disguised as hard work, so most people don't recognize them." – *Quote #30*

5. **Arthur Ashe:** "Start where you are. Use what you have. Do what you can." – *Quote #19*

6. **Ayn Rand:** "The question isn't who is going to let me. It's who is going to stop me." – *Quote #97*

7. **Barack Obama:** "Change will not come if we wait for some other person or some other time. We are the ones we've been waiting for. We are the change that we seek." – *Quote #98*

8. **Bo Bennett:** "Success is not in what you have, but who you are." – *Quote #35*

9. **Bruce Lee:** "The successful warrior is the average man, with laser-like focus." – *Quote #22*

10. **Charles Kingsleigh:** "The only way to achieve the impossible is to believe it is possible." – *Quote #89*
11. **Chris Grosser:** "Opportunities don't happen, you create them." – **Quote #6**

12. **Christian D. Larson:** "Believe in yourself and all that you are. Know that there is something inside you that is greater than any obstacle." – *Quote #72*

13. **Confucius:** "It does not matter how slowly you go as long as you do not stop." – **Quote #51**

14. **C.S. Lewis:** "Hardships often prepare ordinary people for an extraordinary destiny." – **Quote #77**

15. **Eleanor Roosevelt:** "Do one thing every day that scares you." – **Quote #17**

16. **Estée Lauder:** "I never dreamed about success, I worked for it." – **Quote #33**

17. **Frank Sinatra:** "The best revenge is massive success." – **Quote #32**

18. **Franklin D. Roosevelt:** "The only limit to our realization of tomorrow is our doubts of today." – **Quote #10**

19. **George Eliot:** "It's never too late to be what you might have been." – **Quote #76**

20. **George S. Patton:** "Success is how high you bounce when you hit bottom." – **Quote #11**

21. **Gloria Steinem:** "Without leaps of imagination or dreaming, we lose the excitement of possibilities. Dreaming, after all, is a form of planning." – *Quote #92*

22. **Henry David Thoreau**: "Success usually comes to those who are too busy to be looking for it." – *Quote #14*

23. **Ivan Turgenev:** "If we wait for the moment when everything, absolutely everything is ready, we shall never begin." – *Quote #94*

24. **Jim Rohn**: "If you are not willing to risk the usual, you will have to settle for the ordinary." – *Quote #24*

25. **John 14:6**: "I am the way and the truth and the life. No one comes to the Father except through me." – *Quote #63*

26. **John 14:27**: "Peace I leave with you; my peace I give you. I do not give to you as the world gives. Do not let your hearts be troubled and do not be afraid." – *Quote #65*

27. **John 16:33**: "I have told you these things, so that in me you may have peace. In this world you will have trouble. But take heart! I have overcome the world." – *Quote #68*

28. **John 8:12**: "I am the light of the world. Whoever follows me will never walk in darkness, but will have the light of life." – *Quote #66*

29. **John 10:10**: "The thief comes only to steal and kill and destroy; I have come that they may have life, and have it to the full." – *Quote #71*

30. **John D. Rockefeller:** "Don't be afraid to give up the good to go for the great." – *Quote #8*

31. **Jordan Belfort**: "The only thing standing between you and your goal is the story you keep telling yourself as to why you can't achieve it." – *Quote #56*

32. **Julie Andrews:** "Perseverance is failing 19 times and succeeding the 20th." – *Quote #60*

33. **Mahatma Gandhi**: "The future depends on what you do today." – *Quote #2*

34. **Mark Twain**: "The secret of getting ahead is getting started." – *Quote #25*

35. **Matthew 6:25**: "Therefore I tell you, do not worry about your life, what you will eat or drink; or about your body, what you will wear. Is not life more than food, and the body more than clothes?" – **Quote #69**

36. **Matthew 7:7**: "Ask and it will be given to you; seek and you will find; knock and the door will be opened to you." – *Quote #70*

37. **Matthew 11:28:** "Come to me, all you who are weary and burdened, and I will give you rest." – *Quote #62*

38. **Matthew 19:26:** "With man this is impossible, but with God all things are possible." – *Quote #64*

39. **Matthew 28:20:** "And surely I am with you always, to the very end of the age." – *Quote #67*

40. **Maya Angelou:** "You may encounter many defeats, but you must not be defeated. In fact, it may be necessary to encounter the defeats, so you can know who you are, what you can rise from, how you can still come out of it." – *Quote #99*

41. **Milton Berle:** "If opportunity doesn't knock, build a door." – *Quote #31*

42. **M. Scott Peck:** "The truth is that our finest moments are most likely to occur when we are feeling deeply uncomfortable, unhappy or unfulfilled. For it is only in such moments, propelled by our discomfort, that we are likely to step out of our ruts and start searching for different ways or truer answers." – *Quote #96*

43. **Napoleon Hill:** "A goal is a dream with a deadline." – *Quote #49*

44. **Nelson Mandela:** "It always seems impossible until it's done." – *Quote #9*

45. **Nikos Kazantzakis**: "In order to succeed, we must first believe that we can." – *Quote #28*

46. **Norman Vaughan:** "Dream big and dare to fail." – *Quote #13*

47. **Nolan Bushnell:** "Everyone who's ever taken a shower has an idea. It's the person who gets out of the shower, dries off and does something about it who makes a difference." – *Quote #95*

48. **Og Mandino:** "Failure will never overtake me if my determination to succeed is strong enough." – *Quote #84*

49. **Orison Swett Marden:** "Success is not measured by what you accomplish, but by the opposition you have encountered, and the courage with which you have maintained the struggle against overwhelming odds." – *Quote #61*

50. **Pauline Kael:** "Where there is a will, there is a way. If there is a chance in a million that you can do something, anything, to keep what you want from ending, do it. Pry the door open or, if need be, wedge your foot in that door and keep it open." – *Quote #100*

51. **Peter Drucker:** "The best way to predict the future is to create it." – *Quote #12*

52. **Ralph Waldo Emerson:** "What lies behind us and what lies before us are tiny matters compared to what lies within us." – *Quote #80*

53. **Richard Bach:** "You are always free to change your mind and choose a different future, or a different past." – *Quote #93*

54. **Robert Kiyosaki:** "Don't let the fear of losing be greater than the excitement of winning." – *Quote #46*

55. **Sam Levenson:** "Don't watch the clock; do what it does. Keep going." – *Quote #5*

56. **Steve Jobs:** "The only way to do great work is to love what you do." – *Quote #3*

57. **Theodore Roosevelt:** "Believe you can and you're halfway there." – *Quote #4*

58. **Thomas A. Edison:** "Many of life's failures are people who did not realize how close they were to success when they gave up." – *Quote #40*

59. **Thomas Carlyle:** "Go as far as you can see; when you get there, you'll be able to see further." – *Quote #18*

60. **Thomas Jefferson:** "I find that the harder I work, the more luck I seem to have." – *Quote #15*

61. **Thomas Paine:** "The harder the conflict, the more glorious the triumph." – *Quote #90*

62. **Vidal Sassoon:** "The only place where success comes before work is in the dictionary." – *Quote #29*

63. **Vince Lombardi:** "It's not whether you get knocked down, it's whether you get up." – *Quote #87*

64. **Walter Elliot:** "Perseverance is not a long race; it is many short races one after the other." – *Quote #86*

65. **Walt Disney:** "The way to get started is to quit talking and

begin doing." – *Quote #21*

66. **Walt Whitman:** "Keep your face always toward the sunshine—and shadows will fall behind you." – *Quote #36*

67. **Wayne Gretzky:** "You miss 100% of the shots you don't take." – *Quote #47*

68. **Will Rogers:** "Don't let yesterday take up too much of today." – *Quote #20*

69. **William Butler Yeats:** "Do not wait to strike till the iron is hot, but make it hot by striking." – *Quote #46*

70. **William James:** "Act as if what you do makes a difference. It does." – *Quote #81*

71. **Winston Churchill:** "Success is not final, failure is not fatal: It is the courage to continue that counts." – *Quote #1*

72. *Winston S. Churchill:* "Success is stumbling from failure to failure with no loss of enthusiasm." – *Quote #59*

73. **Zig Ziglar:** "You don't have to be great to start, but you have to start to be great." – *Quote #26*

74. **Arthur Ashe:** "Start where you are. Use what you have. Do what you can." – *Quote #19*

75. *Christian D. Larson:* "Believe in yourself and all that you are. Know that there is something inside you that is greater than any obstacle." – *Quote #72*

76. **John D. Rockefeller:** "Don't be afraid to give up the good to go for the great." – *Quote #8*

77. **Julie Andrews:** "Perseverance is failing 19 times and succeeding the 20th." – *Quote #60*

78. **Mahatma Gandhi:** "The future depends on what you do today." – *Quote #2*

79. **Mark Twain:** "The secret of getting ahead is getting started." – *Quote #25*

80. **Matthew 6:25:** "Therefore I tell you, do not worry about your life, what you will eat or drink; or about your body, what you will wear. Is not life more than food, and the body more than clothes?" – *Quote #69*

81. **Matthew 7:7:** "Ask and it will be given to you; seek and you will find; knock and the door will be opened to you." – *Quote #70*

82. **Matthew 11:28:** "Come to me, all you who are weary and burdened, and I will give you rest." – *Quote #62*

83. **Matthew 19:26:** "With man this is impossible, but with God all things are possible." – *Quote #64*

84. **Matthew 28:20:** "And surely I am with you always, to the very end of the age." – *Quote #67*

85. **Maya Angelou:** "You may encounter many defeats, but you must not be defeated. In fact, it may be necessary to encounter the defeats, so you can know who you are, what you can rise from, how you can still come out of it." – **Quote #99**

86. **Milton Berle:** "If opportunity doesn't knock, build a door." – *Quote #31*

87. **M. Scott Peck:** "The truth is that our finest moments are most likely to occur when we are feeling deeply uncomfortable,

unhappy or unfulfilled. For it is only in such moments, propelled by our discomfort, that we are likely to step out of our ruts and start searching for different ways or truer answers." – ***Quote #96***

88. **Napoleon Hill:** "A goal is a dream with a deadline." – ***Quote #49***

89. **Nelson Mandela**: "It always seems impossible until it's done." – ***Quote #9***

90. **Nikos Kazantzakis:** "In order to succeed, we must first believe that we can." – ***Quote #28***

91. **Norman Vaughan:** "Dream big and dare to fail." – ***Quote #13***

92. **Nolan Bushnell:** "Everyone who's ever taken a shower has an idea. It's the person who gets out of the shower, dries off and does something about it who makes a difference." – ***Quote #95***

93. **Og Mandino:** "Failure will never overtake me if my determination to succeed is strong enough." – ***Quote #84***

94. **Orison Swett Marden**: "Success is not measured by what you accomplish, but by the opposition you have encountered, and the courage with which you have maintained the struggle against overwhelming odds." – ***Quote #61***

95. **Pauline Kael:** "Where there is a will, there is a way. If there is a chance in a million that you can do something, anything, to keep what you want from ending, do it. Pry the door open or, if need be, wedge your foot in that door and keep it open." – ***Quote #100***

96. **Peter Drucker:** "The best way to predict the future is to create it." – ***Quote #12***

97. **Ralph Waldo Emerson:** "What lies behind us and what lies before us are tiny matters compared to what lies within us." –

Quote #80

98. **Richard Bach:** "You are always free to change your mind and choose a different future, or a different past." – *Quote #93*

99. **Robert Kiyosaki:** "Don't let the fear of losing be greater than the excitement of winning." – *Quote #46*

100. **Sam Levenson:** "Don't watch the clock; do what it does. Keep going." – *Quote #5*

ACKNOWLEDGMENTS

◆ ◆ ◆

I would like to thank my family, friends, and mentors for their unwavering support and encouragement during my job search journey. Your belief in me made all the difference. Thanks to my husband, daughter, and mother-in-law; they really are my backbone to continue moving on. I have learned a lot during this time, and their emotional support is more than important.

ABOUT THE AUTHOR

Miriam Figueroa

She is a distinguished Database Admin/Software Engineer and Cloud Architect with over 20 years of impactful experience in both Government and e-commerce sectors. She holds an impressive academic background with a Master of Computer Science from Florida Atlantic University, a Master of Engineering Applied to Engineering and Architecture, and a B.Sc. in Computer Science.

Miriam's expertise spans multiple domains, including database administration (MySQL, PostgreSQL, MariaDB, Oracle, MongoDB, MSSQL, Snowflake, CosmosDB, ClickHouse, Azure, and AWS), data engineering, ETL pipelines, and project management. Her technical prowess is backed by a suite of prestigious certifications: Microsoft Certified Azure Administrator Associate, Azure Data Engineer Associate, Azure Database Administrator Associate, and Azure Solutions Architect Expert.

Driven by her personal journey through the challenges of job searching, Miriam decided to compile this book to provide practical advice and sustained motivation to fellow job seekers. Her deep understanding of the industry's demands and the job market's intricacies positions her as a valuable guide. Through this book, she aims to inspire and equip readers with the resilience and tools needed to navigate their career paths successfully.

Connect with Miriam on LinkedIn:https://www.linkedin/in/miriam-figueroa-alfonso

www.ingramcontent.com/pod-product-compliance
Lightning Source LLC
Chambersburg PA
CBHW071507220526
45472CB00003B/947